The
Official Book of Me

The
Official Book of Me

TIPS FOR A LIFESTYLE OF HEALTH, HAPPINESS & WELLNESS

by Marlene Wallach

With Grace Norwich

Illustrated by Monika Roe

Previously published individually
as *My Self* and *My Life*

Aladdin

NEW YORK • LONDON • TORONTO • SYDNEY • NEW DELHI

☜ Aladdin

An imprint of Simon & Schuster Children's Publishing Division

1230 Avenue of the Americas, New York, NY 10020

This Aladdin paperback edition December 2013

My Self text copyright © 2009 by Marlene Wallach

My Life text copyright © 2009 by Marlene Wallach

Interior illustrations copyright © 2009 by Monika Roe

Cover illustration copyright © 2013 by Annabelle Metayer

All rights reserved, including the right of reproduction in whole or in part in any form.

Aladdin is a trademark of Simon & Schuster, Inc., and related logo is a registered trademark of Simon & Schuster, Inc.

Material was originally published individually in *My Self: A Guide to Me* and *My Life: A Guide to Health & Fitness*

For information about special discounts for bulk purchases, please contact Simon & Schuster Special Sales at 1-866-506-1949 or business@simonandschuster.com.

The Simon & Schuster Speakers Bureau can bring authors to your live event. For more information or to book an event contact the Simon & Schuster Speakers Bureau at 1-866-248-3049 or visit our website at www.simonspeakers.com.

Designed by Jeanine Henderson and Karin Paprocki

The text of this book was set in ITC Avant Garde Gothic.

Manufactured in the United States

10 9 8 7 6 5 4 3

Library of Congress Control Number 2013932678

ISBN 978-1-4424-9479-4

ISBN 978-1-4424-9480-0 (eBook)

0214 RR2

Anna is a fourteen-year-old gymnast I met after her six months in a full-body cast, during her two years of physical therapy, all the result of a serious car accident. It is hard to believe that after all she went through, she is now on track for the upcoming Olympics. This book is dedicated to Anna, whose courage and beauty of spirit will inspire me for the rest of my life.

CONTENTS

�֍   �֍   ✖

introduction

THE OFFICIAL BOOK OF ME IS A GUIDE for *you*! Yes, *you*—that means it's okay to flip through the pages, only answer the quizzes, check out just the parts that interest you, maybe read about the things you are not familiar with, or read the book in the traditional way from beginning to end. This book is a resource you can refer to for a lifetime.

Staying fit and eating healthy are things everyone wants to learn more about. You can always refer to this book to find a new sport or physical activity. And when do you ever stop wanting to feel good about yourself and learn new ways to help your inner beauty shine through or explore your spirituality? I refer to all these things as your *wellness*. Wellness includes everything about your physical, emotional, spiritual, and intellectual self . . . in short, your life.

The first part of the book deals with getting and staying fit. There are different options presented for physical fitness and sports, tips on eating right and sleeping enough, and fun facts and quizzes. It's filled with practical advice and easy-to-follow steps that will help to guide you through a healthy day from the time you wake up in the morning to the time your head hits the pillow at night. You'll learn that no matter what you see on TV or read in magazines, there is no such thing as *perfect*. No perfect body, no perfect food, no perfect exercise. Maybe this isn't what you want to learn about at the moment or what you enjoy reading about, but regardless, it is there for when you are in the mood for tuning in to your health.

The second part of the book deals a lot with feelings, which we know are not black and white. You are a best friend, a daughter, a student, maybe a trendsetter, maybe a thrill seeker—how do you handle all this and not go insane? How do you help your unique beauty and personality shine through so that others can see how truly amazing you are? In this book, you'll read about how you can deal with these issues, and you'll find lots of tips and advice—everything you need to know to begin feeling self-confident and free to express yourself in your daily life.

And of course the two parts of this book cross over. We have all heard about how a good attitude and a positive outlook (emotional) can help cure certain illnesses (physical) and how when you feel good about yourself (emotional) you look good too (physical). An overall message of the book is that a good attitude helps with everything!

Being a girl today is terrific, terrifying, wonderful, and wacky—all at the same time. *The Official Book of Me* is here to help you learn how to live your amazing life to the fullest. So here we go. You'll see—there's a lot to learn.

chapter 1
KEEPING FIT

GET PUMPED

A BODY IN MOTION TENDS TO STAY in motion. Have you learned that yet in science class? This law of physics goes for people, too! If you're physically active—dancing, jumping rope, playing sports, even just walking to a friend's house—your body will respond by being a lot more energetic. And the more energy you have, the more ready you'll be to tackle all the things that come up throughout the course of your day.

Before we begin, it's important to know that exercise is already a part of your day, probably much more than you think. You go to school, right? You go up and down the steps, right? BINGO—you're exercising. Do you ride a bike to a friend's house, run an errand, or walk the dog? That's exercise. Dance in your room or with your friends? That's exercise too. Let's explore ways to make exercise a fun part of your everyday routine.

THE LOWDOWN
ON EXERCISE

EXERCISE CAN BE DIVIDED INTO two basic categories: cardiovascular and strength training. Cardiovascular is all about getting your heart rate up. It involves breaking a sweat for thirty minutes or longer, by going for a long jog or swimming laps, for example.

Strength training is designed to build muscle and tone your body. Lifting weights is the most popular form of strength training, but it's not the only one. Yoga is also a form of strength training.

The goal is to come up with a routine that balances both kinds of exercise—one that you really enjoy. That way you'll have a healthy heart and good muscle tone, and you'll be a very happy person. Exercise is an important part of feeling good in both mind and body. Once you make exercise a part of your routine, you'll notice how your mood improves every time you do it. "Sound body, sound mind" is how fitness experts describe the benefits of exercise.

NO GYM EQUIPMENT?
NO EXCUSE!

A JUMP ROPE CAN ACT AS A GREAT piece of equipment for a variety of exercises.

- Hold one end of the rope in each hand and raise your hands over your head. Bend at the

waist from side to side, stretching your waist and your arms.

- Hold one end of the rope in each hand and stretch your legs in the loop, one at a time.

- Jump rope and get your aerobic exercise. Skip rope down the street and see how quickly you get out of breath. Double Dutch with friends so your arms get a work-out when it's not your turn to jump. Then you jump twice as much when it's your turn.

RIDING A BIKE IS TERRIFIC EXERCISE— and it's a great mode of transportation. Please remember that a helmet is always a must! If you find long rides uncomfortable, special padded bike shorts are available in most sporting goods stores.

Quiz: Activity Meter

Some people are natural-born athletes. Others are natural-born couch potatoes. Then there are those who are in between. Which are you? Take this quiz to see which group you fall into.

1. **Your idea of the perfect way to spend a sunny weekend afternoon is:**

    A. going to the movies with friends (1 point)

    B. playing in an all-day tournament with your favorite sports team (3 points)

    C. spending the day in the park (2 points)

2. **If you were a car, you would be:**

    A. a sport utility vehicle (3 points)

    B. a hybrid (2 points)

C. a convertible (1 point)

3. Your favorite thing to watch on TV is:

A. nature shows (2 points)

B. music videos (1 point)

C. professional sports (3 points)

4. During lunchtime, you:

A. head straight to chat with friends (1 point)

B. go for a long walk around the school to collect your thoughts (2 points)

C. run straight to the school yard for Double Dutch (3 points)

5. A good workout for you is:

A. riding your bike (3 points)

B. gym class (2 points)

C. jogging to the refrigerator during a commercial break (1 point)

6. When you are assigned a school project, you work best:

A. alone (1 point)

B. with one other person (2 points)

C. with the entire class (3 points)

7. **Your favorite shoes are:**

A. ballet flats (2 points)

B. flip-flops (1 point)

C. running sneakers (3 points)

8. **While playing a board game with your family:**

A. you'll do whatever it takes to win (3 points)

B. you would be the one in charge of the snacks (1 point)

C. it doesn't matter who wins or loses, you just want to have fun (2 points)

9. **If you could drink only one thing, it would be:**

A. tea (2 points)

B. soda (1 point)

C. water (3 points)

10. Nothing says vacation like:

   A. a week on the beach, catching up on your favorite mags (1 point)

   B. a white-water rafting adventure on the hardest rapids around (3 points)

   C. a camping trip with hiking and s'mores (2 points)

If you scored . . .

10-17 points:

YOU ARE THE MOST LAID-BACK PERSON around. You're serious about relaxation. Sports and sweating are not high priorities on your to-do list. Your easygoing attitude makes you fun to be around, but you need to work on your workout. Look for activities such as softball that combine sports with socializing. You may soon find yourself running around a track! Try other group and social sports like bowling and soccer.

18–24 points:

YOU LOVE TO GET YOUR BLOOD PUMPING WITH A fast-paced walk or a friendly game with your neighbors. Super-competitive sports just aren't your thing. That's okay. You get lots of exercise while still maintaining your Zen approach. Don't be afraid to push yourself now and then by trying team sports. You'd make a great team member!

25–30 points:

NOTHING AND NO ONE CAN SLOW YOU DOWN. Your high energy fuels everything you do. If there's a ball around, you want to hit it. If there's a game going on, you want to join in. That means you are super-fit, which is great. Please don't forget to take it easy so you don't get hurt. Remember to stretch, cool down, and drink lots of water. And when your mom tells you to come inside from your game, listen to her!

GET IN THE GAME

THE HEALTH BENEFITS YOU GET FROM sports and exercise stay with you for your whole life. Would you believe muscles have memory, too? If you learn tennis at age twelve, you'll be able to pick up that racquet again very easily at age eighteen, even if you haven't played much in the six years in between!

There are lots of sports and activities you can try, not all of them with a team. Running and biking are solo sports. Don't forget that dancing gets the heart pumping too. Sports you can play with a pal include tennis and Ping-Pong.

BASIC SKILLS: HOW DO YOU MEASURE UP?

DIFFERENT SPORTS CALL FOR DIFferent skills, but there are some basics that any physical activity requires: flexibility, balance, stamina, coordination, strength, speed, and agility.

Take this quick test to see how you rate in each of these categories. After each activity, give yourself a score of 1 to 10 (1 is the lowest and 10 the highest). The higher you score, the better you are at that activity.

Stamina: Do twenty jumping jacks. As soon as you finish, recite the Pledge of Allegiance._____

Coordination: Pat your head, rub your tummy, and recite the alphabet all at the same time._____

Strength: Lift your backpack filled with your schoolbooks over your head ten times._____

Flexibility: While standing, bend and touch your toes ten times._____

Balance: Walk along a straight line, putting one foot in front of the other._____

THE WIDE WORLD OF SPORTS

NOW THAT YOU KNOW WHAT YOUR strengths are, explore the following options. Trying different sports not only keeps exercise interesting, but it also challenges you to use your body in different ways. So whether you love all kinds of workouts, or you've never found a sport you're passionate about, check out the chart on the following pages to find an activity that is perfect for you.

Activity	About	Cardiovascular Value
Basketball	This popular team sport can also be played one-on-one.	HIGH, especially if you're playing a full-court match.
Bicycling	Not only is cycling a great form of exercise, it's an efficient way to get from point A to point B.	EXTREMELY HIGH. Riding a bike is an excellent aerobic exercise, and it puts very little stress on the joints.
Dancing	There are countless ways to work up a sweat on the dance floor, from salsa to square dancing.	EXTREMELY HIGH, as long as you don't take too many breaks.

MODERATE. Shooting hoops works the arms, and all the jumping is great for the legs.

Doing passing drills with a medicine ball, which is heavier than a basketball, is a great way to develop arm and upper-body strength.

HIGH. Especially good for the legs and gluteus maximus (otherwise known as the butt muscle).

Remember to take water along when you ride, as well as an air pump. You don't want a flat tire to ruin your workout. There are pumps that fasten to your bike, so you don't have to worry about carrying one in your pocket.

HIGH. Dancing is a great workout for the lower body. It's no wonder dancers are known for their great legs!

As with any sport, stretching is essential before hitting the dance floor. Pay special attention to hip and butt muscles, which are prone to injury when dancing.

Activity	About	Cardiovascular Value
Rollerblading	Also known as in-line skating, it's a relative of traditional roller skating.	EXTREMELY HIGH. It might look recreational but Rollerblading can raise the heart rate nearly as high as running and cycling.
Running	This ancient form of exercise is still going strong after thousands of years.	EXTREMELY HIGH. There's no faster way to a healthy heart.
Soccer	Possibly the most popular team sport in the world, soccer is played by both boys and girls in the United States.	MODERATE to HIGH, depending on how much the ball is in play and how close you are to the action.

Strengthening Value	Expert Tip

HIGH. Your leg and butt muscles will be superfirm after a few months on Rollerblades, especially if you add some hills into your routine.

Location is key when learning to Rollerblade. Choose a paved surface with few people around. Empty basketball courts and vacant parking lots are two good options.

• •

HIGH. Works the leg muscles and helps develop the upper body, too.

To prevent injury, replace your running shoes approximately every 350 miles.

• •

IT DEPENDS. If you're the goalie, soccer is great for upper body. If you play any other position, this is a great workout for your lower body, because you'll be running and kicking a lot.

Soccer is a game with lots of stops and starts. To be in top shape for this sport, practice your sprints—running at full speed for short distances.

Activity	About	Cardiovascular Value
Skiing	Whether downhill or cross-country, this winter sport combines fun and fitness with the great outdoors.	HIGH to EXTREMELY HIGH. Cross-country skiing is up there with running. But downhill skiing is surprisingly strenuous too.
Swimming	Not only is swimming a great form of exercise, it prepares you for all sorts of water sports, from sailing to waterskiing.	HIGH. You won't notice all the sweat pouring out your body, but swimming can burn as many calories as other forms of aerobic exercise.
Yoga	Yoga began five thousand years ago in India as a spiritual practice, but it's now a form of exercise practiced the world over.	MODERATE. Yoga mainly involves slow to moderate-paced move-ments, but it still gives your heart a pretty good workout.

Strengthening Value	Expert Tip
HIGH. No burn in the legs rivals what you feel after a day on the slopes—especially if the trails are flat.	Whether it's your first time on skis or your hundredth, always wear a helmet to protect your head from injury.
HIGH. Swimming uses all the major muscle groups, especially if you do all the main strokes, which include freestyle, butterfly, breast, and the backstroke.	Swimming has zero impact on the joints, so it's the most injury-free sport there is. That means you can do it everyday. Because you are sweating while swimming, keep a water bottle handy.
HIGH. By holding the many yoga postures or paced movements, your entire body will get stronger and more limber. With some poses, you are weight-lifting yourself!	It may not be a contact sport, but yoga can lead to serious injury. That's why it's important to begin with a trained instructor who will start you out with safe, low-impact poses.

Quiz: Sports Trivia

Test your sports savvy!

✳ ✳ ✳

Which phrase best describes each sport below? Draw a line to connect them.

Yoga   Can play one-on-one

Skiing   Should wear knee pads

Basketball   May end up with helmet hair

Dancing   Ancient form of exercise

Soccer   Prone to hip injuries

Running   Prepares you for sailing

Rollerblading   Five thousand years old

Swimming   Cross-country is one kind

Biking   World-renowned sport

ON YOUR MARK, GET SET— WAIT A MINUTE

WHAT A LOT OF US FORGET TO do before we start an activity or sport is warm up properly—or warm up at all! It's important to get blood flowing to those muscles of yours before you start to exercise. Do the activity you're warming up for, but really slowly to get your muscles ready. For example, if you're going to dance, begin by stretching your legs and arms and dancing in slow motion. Or walk for five minutes before you start jogging.

A light warm-up loosens your joints and makes you more agile for whatever you're going to do. It also gives you time to get mentally prepared for the physical challenge—getting "pumped up," as some athletes call it.

Don't forget to stretch *after* you exercise too. This

"cool-down" will help you to enjoy the rest of the day injury free.

QUICK HEART-TO-HEART

HOW EFFICIENTLY ARE YOU EXERcising? Pro athletes use something called "target heart rate" to measure their fitness level during exercise. You can spend a lot of money on a monitor to track your heart rate, but there's an easier way to figure out how hard you're working, and it doesn't cost a thing. It's called finding your *zone*. Do your favorite activity at increasing levels of intensity to get a sense of what each feels like. Normally, you'll want to stay within the moderate to aerobic zones.

Warm-up Zone: This means you are able to sing a song while you exercise.

Moderate Zone: You can talk easily while you exercise.

Aerobic Zone: It gets harder to talk while you exercise.

Anaerobic Zone: You are no longer able to talk while you exercise.

Redline Zone: Time to stop when you're gasping for air.

It's Cool to Sweat!

SWEATING SOMETIMES GETS A BAD reputation, but it's the most natural thing in the world. In fact, sweat is the body's natural cooling system. When your body gets hotter than the normal 98.6 degrees, the part of the brain that controls temperature responds by telling your body's sweat glands to release some moisture through tiny openings in the skin, called pores. Once the sweat hits the air it evaporates, and that cools down your body. This is why it's so important to drink a lot of water when you exercise. You need to replace the fluids that are lost when your body sweats.

NO PAIN, NO GAIN?

**D**ON'T LIKE SPORTS, BUT WANT to exercise? Here are some activities that'll help whip you into shape. Look at this list and number them in order, favorites first.

_____ Jumping rope

_____ Dancing around your room

_____ Raking leaves

_____ Watering the garden

_____ Swinging on a swing

_____ Walking with the dog or playing with pets

_____ Shoveling snow

_____ Washing the car (a good way to earn some extra money, too!)

To help you get going, first pick a start date. Then write the dates you plan to start your top three activities

and stick to making daily exercise a fun part of your
routine:

1._____

2._____

3._____

WALK THIS WAY, PLEASE

W ALKING IS ONE OF THE
oldest and best forms of exercise.
There are tons of benefits:

1. You can do it anywhere and with anyone—including
   in the mall with friends!
2. Walking doesn't require a lot of expensive equipment
   beyond a good pair of sneakers.
3. Walking is a low-impact activity, so it doesn't usually
   cause injury.

4. Walking may not seem as intense as other activities, but it's a great way to get your heart pumping.

Here are a few tips for making the most of this popular activity:

- Chin up: Just like models on the catwalk, it's important to maintain proper posture when you're walking for exercise. Try to hold your head erect (but don't forget to look down to see what's in front of you on the ground), and keep your back and stomach as flat as possible. Swing your arms, too. This helps create a faster heartbeat, doubling the cardiovascular benefit. "Cardio" refers to your heart and "vascular" to your blood vessels.
- Multitask: While you're walking is a great time to get things done. You can return a call to a gal pal or listen to a podcast. If you walk with a friend, you can quiz each other for an upcoming test.
- Make a playlist: Listening to music makes the time fly.

Mix it up, using fast dance tunes and slower music for taking a breather. Walk around a track or through a very well-traveled or well-lit park if you can. It's safer than the street, where there's traffic.

GOOD POSTURE ALL DAY

GOOD POSTURE IS IMPORTANT throughout the day, especially when you're sitting in school and at home. You use computers at school to work on projects. When you get back home, you surf the Internet and do your homework on your laptop. Then you spend hours IMing the latest news with friends. In the car, you keep up with countless texts. That's a lot of time typing and being hunched over! Technology can cause a strain on your body, but it doesn't have to if you maintain the correct position. Try these suggestions:

- **Peak Position:** Ideally, you should sit in a good chair with back support when at the computer. Avoid slumping forward and crossing your legs for long periods of time. Sit with the screen at eye level to keep from craning your neck.

- **Hold It:** Switch the hand using the mouse once in a while. Type or move the mouse with straight, loose wrists.

- **Time Limit:** Look away from the screen every ten minutes or so and take a full break by standing up every thirty minutes or so. Stretch, run in place, or take a quick drink of water. When you come back, you'll be amazed how much faster you can read or write.

DON'T LET GERMS
MAKE YOU SICK

GYM CLASS WILL HELP KEEP YOU healthy, but not if you pick up a cold while you're working out. Germs can be transmitted through sweat, so it's important to take a few extra precautions before you pick up those dumbbells.

- Wash your hands before and after you work out. While in gym class, don't put your fingers near your eyes, nose, or mouth, the most vulnerable parts of your body in terms of germs.

- Have someone with clean hands help you if you get a cut. Clean the cut with an antibiotic ointment and use a Band-Aid.

33

- Don't share gym clothes, towels, or any other personal items with friends, since bacteria can live on fabric for almost three months!
- Use soap from dispensers, not bars, when showering after a workout. If your school gym doesn't offer them, bring your own soap in a pump bottle.

SPIC-AND-SPAN

THERE'S NO DOUBT ABOUT IT: EXERcise can make you sweaty and dirty, especially if you play an outdoor team sport like soccer or field hockey. It's not possible to shower every time you break a sweat, but you at least want to wash your hands after gym or practice is over or when you come in from outside. Dirty hands transmit colds, the flu, and other bugs. Here's how to go about a serious hand wash:

1. Wet your hands under warm water and lather them up with soap.

2. Scrub your hands and wrists for twenty seconds (that's about as long as it takes to sing the "Happy Birthday" song).

3. Rinse well.

4. Dry off with a paper towel and use the same towel to turn off the faucet and open the door. Then toss the towel in the trash.

LIFE'S A GYM

YOU DON'T HAVE TO BE IN A GYM or a health club to exercise. There are plenty of everyday items around your house that can be used with exercises. Here are just a few examples.

- **Water bottles:** Use plastic water bottles instead of weights. Start out with half-liter bottles in each hand and curl them toward your shoulders to work on your biceps. Move up to one-liter bottles as you get stronger.

- **Bathrobe belt:** A cloth belt makes the perfect stretching band. Sit on the floor with one leg out and the other bent against the ground. Put the belt around the foot that's outstretched and hold on to the ends with your hands to stretch your hamstrings. The farther down you hold the belt, the more stretch you'll get.

- **Staircase:** This is the original Stairmaster! There's no better way to get a cardiovascular workout and strengthen your butt and thigh muscles than to run up and down the stairs.

※   ※   ※

MOVE IT

SPORTS AND EXERCISE ARE GREAT for you, and it's important to make them a regular part of your life. Whether you're a natural athlete or not, getting the blood pumping and working those muscles will make your body stronger and your soul soar.

chapter 2
GOOD EATING

FOOD IS THE FUEL FOR LIFE AND living—24/7. The saying goes, "Garbage in, garbage out." If you put a lot of unhealthy fuel into your body, you're not going to have the energy to race around the way you want to. It's important to eat food loaded with vitamins and minerals as much as possible so that you'll have enough energy to fire you through a super-busy day. It's critical for everyone to get the vitamins found in healthy foods, and it's especially true for young people, so that everything from your bones to your brain can develop to its full potential.

FOOD, GLORIOUS FOOD

What Is a Processed Food?

YOU MAY HAVE HEARD PEOPLE TALK ABOUT processed food in a bad way. Processed foods get a bad rap, but the truth is that certain processed foods *are* good for you. Milk is one example. Simply put, processed food is food that has been changed from its original state through an artificial process. In the case of milk, it's pasteurization. Pasteurization is a process of heating milk to kill off harmful bacteria. That's an artificial process, but it's a good thing.

If that's an artificial process, what's a natural process? An example of a natural process is a tomato growing on a vine, turning from green to red as it ripens.

A lot of food is processed more than it needs to be, and that is the kind of food that is not healthy for you. Foods with too much added salt, sugar, fat, or chemicals can be described as "overprocessed" and should be eaten in limited quantities, if at all. Certain cheeses, sandwich meats, hot dogs, and lots of fast foods are examples of food that is overprocessed.

Healthy Choices

WHEN YOU GO WITH YOUR MOM OR DAD TO the supermarket, don't walk by the frozen food aisle! Frozen foods are not just a convenience; frozen fruits and veggies can be just as healthy as fresh foods. Food nowadays is frozen at its peak of freshness, right after it's picked, by a process called "flash freezing," which is just another way of saying it's frozen really quickly to lock in the flavor and the nutrients. Flash freezing is done so quickly that no chemicals or preservatives are needed.

Do your parents tell you all the time to eat your veggies and drink your milk? They're onto something! Milk is loaded with just about all the ingredients a growing body needs. Unfortunately, a lot of girls don't drink milk, and then they don't get the calcium they need in order to build strong bones, the iron for healthy muscles, or zinc for overall development. If you don't like milk, try low-fat yogurt or cheese for the same healthy nutrients.

There's no shortage of food in the United States, but with all the fast-food restaurants and overprocessed products that are around, it's sometimes hard to make the right choices. But don't worry. It's easy to improve your nutrition if you want to. It's not about finding the "perfect" diet—no such thing exists. It's being smart about what you put into your body and feeling great with the results. One of the basics to remember about nearly everything in life, including food, is the idea of *moderation*. You can have just about anything you want if you don't eat too much.

Now let's learn what it really takes to fuel you up!

What's All This Talk About Calories and Why Do I Care?

CALORIES ARE A MEASURE OF HOW much energy is in a food. If you don't eat enough calories, you won't have enough energy to get you through the day. Because people come in all shapes and sizes and because everyone exercises at different levels, the number of calories you need can range from 1,600 to 2,500 calories. Your doctor can advise you as to how many calories per day you need. You burn calories when walking and playing sports, and your body needs energy for breathing in and out and to keep your heart pumping. And calories—meaning good nutrition—are needed so your body can grow and develop.

THE BASICS

NOW IT'S TIME TO LEARN THE WHO, WHAT, WHERE, and WHEN of healthy eating.

Who

WHOM YOU EAT WITH IS ALMOST AS IMPORTant as what you eat. Eating with others usually slows down the speed with which you gulp down your food. Studies show that sitting down with your family to eat a meal together is good for your body and your soul. If you don't usually eat with your family, talk to a parent about scheduling a family meal one day a week. Try it for the next four weeks, and see if you notice a difference in how you feel!

Maybe if you offer to help your mom or dad prepare the meal, that can become another part of the routine of eating together. It's a nice thing to do and will be much appreciated. Your part can be as simple as setting the table or helping select a healthy menu. For some of you, it might be going shopping with your mom on the way home from school. Whatever it is, be a part of it. Believe it or not, there are claims that being involved in preparing the meal can make the food taste better, so here's a mealtime planner to help you get started. Plan ahead and preparation will be a snap.

Mealtime Planner

WEEK ONE

Date:

Time:

Menu:

WEEK TWO

Date:

Time:

Menu:

WEEK THREE

Date:

Time:

Menu:

WEEK FOUR

Date:

Time:

Menu:

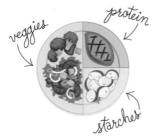

veggies

protein

starches

What

Use this food formula to figure out how your plate should look:

- ½ veggies

- ¼ grains or starchy veggies such as potatoes

- ¼ protein (see "Good Food Glossary" on page 49 for the definition of protein)

Your plate should be colorful as well as balanced.

Where

THE BEST PLACE TO EAT IS AT A TABLE WITH a plate, fork, knife, and napkin. Oops—don't forget a spoon for soup night! Do you inhale your breakfast on the bus to school? You'll enjoy your food much more if you take a minute to stop, sit down, and eat. Try to avoid eating in your bedroom, in front of the TV, or in the car—unless it's just a snack. Eat your meals seated in the kitchen or dining room whenever possible. Exceptions are okay, of course. No one expects you to give up munching popcorn at the movies!

TOP TABLE TALK

It's easy to be a star at the dining room table. Follow these simple rules, and you'll have the best table manners around.

- Wait until everyone is seated before eating. It's also good to wait until three people have been served to dig in.
- To cut your food, hold your fork in your left hand and knife in your right. This may take some practice.
- Ask people to pass anything on the table if it's out of reach.
- Don't talk with your mouth full. Of course you know this, but it doesn't hurt to be reminded!
- It's nice to compliment the cook. If it happens that

you didn't enjoy the meal, you can tell your host or hostess you loved the centerpiece—or you can just thank him or her for a lovely evening.

- It's a very nice thing to offer to help clear the table— and it's good exercise, too!

When

IT'S EASIER TO KEEP A HEALTHY DIET WHEN you eat on a regular schedule. It's not always within your control, of course, but a good daily schedule to try for includes three meals and two snacks. Breakfast is the most important meal and sets the tone for the rest of the day. After all, you haven't eaten in eight or nine hours. It's time to jump-start your brain and give your body energy, so EAT! Sometimes a full tummy when you go to sleep can give you a stomachache, so when possible, eat dinner between six and eight o'clock and try to leave about three hours between your last meal and when you go to sleep.

GOOD FOOD GLOSSARY

THERE ARE SIX KINDS OF NUTRIENTS found in food. They're what's needed to keep everything running smoothly in your body.

Protein

PROTEIN MAKES UP A BIG PART OF YOUR muscles, organs, and even cells. Eat protein regularly to make sure all the organs of your body are properly nourished. Fish, meat, dairy products, and eggs are all excellent sources of protein. There are vegetarian sources of protein too, like tofu, lentils, and beans.

Carbohydrates

YOU MIGHT HAVE HEARD THEM REFERRED to as "carbs." They're made up of sugars used by the body to create energy. Simple carbohydrates include some healthy choices such as milk and many kinds of fruit, like oranges and apples. Simple carbs also include sugars that are bad for you, such as sodas, cake, and candy. The complex kind of carbohydrates, also called starches or fiber, are in whole grains, pasta, beans, and some vegetables like broccoli. Simple carbs give you quick energy and complex carbs give you energy for a longer period of time. Runners often have a large bowl of pasta the evening before they run a marathon because the energy (calories) not used is stored in their body overnight and sustains them during their long run the next day.

Fat

FAT HAS BEEN GIVEN A BAD RAP, BUT IN THE right form, it's an essential part of your diet. It's a part of every cell in your body and provides stored-up energy to use when you miss a meal. Not all forms of fat are healthy. Good sources are olive oil, fish (such as salmon) that has omega-3 fatty acids, avocados, nuts, and seeds. Be sure some "good fat" is a regular part of your diet. Think about substituting the "bad fats"— saturated fats found in meats, poultry, and full-fat dairy products—in your diet with "good fats."

Vitamins

OUR BODIES USE VITAMINS FOR EVERYTHING from building blood cells to repairing injuries. You can get all the vitamins you need from a well-balanced diet, but a multivitamin is always a good way to make sure you get at least the recommended daily dosage. There is nearly an entire alphabet of vitamins. Here are a few.

Vitamin A is important for eyes and skin and can be found in sweet potatoes, carrots, egg yolks, cantaloupe, apricots, and yogurt.

Vitamin B, essential for building cells and giving the body energy, is present in many whole-grain cereals, meat, eggs, and green vegetables. There are several forms of Vitamin B, and each one serves a specific purpose.

Vitamin C, which works to fight infections and strengthen muscles and gums, is found in citrus fruits and tomatoes, and vegetables such as broccoli and red peppers.

Vitamin D is necessary for strong bones and teeth and is found in milk, salmon, and tuna fish. Vitamin D is also found in sunshine!

Vitamin E is helpful in healing wounds and building up your body's strength and is found in whole grains such as oats and wheat, nuts, seeds, and leafy green veggies.

Minerals

MINERALS CONTAIN CHEMICALS THAT HELP with many processes in your body but don't have any calories. Calcium is a very important mineral for young people, especially girls, in order to build strong bones. Calcium is found in milk, spinach, and broccoli. Iron is another important mineral, and it's found in red meat and beans. Other minerals are potassium and zinc.

Water

WATER, WATER, WATER. WE'RE ALWAYS hearing about water and how important it is for health and beauty. Did you know that water covers about 70 percent of the planet? And that your body is made up mostly of water, so you need to replace what you lose from sweating and going to the bathroom. When you exercise or when it's hot out, you use up even more water. Kids should drink six to eight glasses of water each day, and they should try to drink half that amount in school. Carrying a water bottle can be helpful. For more on water, go to page 65.

READING THE FINE PRINT: HOW TO READ FOOD LABELS

NOT ALL FOODS ARE CREATED equal. As you are learning, some are better for you than others. Luckily, there's a nutrition label on every food product to help you make smart choices. It's good to know exactly what you're putting into your body. Here are some tips for reading ingredient and nutrition labels.

What to Look For

1. Read the ingredients list. Every label lists all the ingredients found in the food, starting with the largest

amount and ending with the smallest. If you're looking at an ingredients list for bread, the first ingredient will probably be wheat and one of the last might
be salt.

2. Look at the serving size. The Nutrition Facts label
on your jar or package of food will list how big one
serving is and how many servings are in the package
or jar. The nutritional information that follows is for one
serving, which is measured in cups/grams or pieces.
When comparing two similar products, be sure to
note if the serving size is the same; if not, the values
are not equal.

3. Count the calories. This number tells you how many
calories are in one serving. There is a separate listing
for the amount of calories from fat. Kids caloric needs
range from 1,600 to 2,500 calories. Don't forget to consult

your doctor when you go for your next checkup about how many calories a day you should be eating.

4. Beware these ingredients. Too much fat—saturated fat and trans fat—is not good for your health. Try to limit fat, as well as sugar and salt, in your food. Look for these items as last or close to last on the ingredients list. It's always okay if it's something you love to eat—just eat it in moderation.

5. Figure out the sugars and fiber. This refers to the number of carbohydrate grams in the food. They are broken down into two categories—fiber and sugars. Ideal are foods that have three grams of fiber or more per serving.

6. Protein power. This number tells you the grams of protein in a serving. This is what bodybuilders look

for in order to build strong muscles—and you want to build strong muscles too.

7. The percent daily value (PDV). These are estimates based on a 2,000-calorie-a-day diet for adults, so use these percentage values just to tell whether a food is high or low in nutrients. Here's the rule of thumb:

Low = 5 percent or less of the PDV

High = 20 percent or more of the PDV

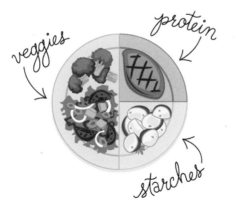

Quiz: What's in Your Food?

Test how well you can read food labels.

❄   ❄   ❄

Nutrition Facts

Serving Size ½ (114g)
Servings Per Container 4

Amount Per Serving

Calories 90   Calories from Fat 30

	% Daily Value*
Total Fat 3g	**5%**
Saturated Fat 0g	**0%**
Cholesterol 0mg	**0%**
Sodium 300mg	**13%**
Total Carbohydrate 13g	**4%**
Dietary Fiber 3g	**12%**
Sugars 3g	
Protein 3g	

Vitamin A	80%	•	Vitamin C	60%
Calcium	4%	•	Iron	4%

---

* Percent Daily Values are based on a 2,000 calorie diet.
Your daily values may be higher or lower depending on
your calorie needs.

1. **How many calories are there in a serving?**

Answer: _____

2. **How many calories are there per package?**

Answer: _____

3. **Is this food item high in fat?**

Answer: _____

4. **How many servings are there in the package?**

Answer: _____

5. **Is this food high in Vitamin A?**

Answer: _____

LET'S GET COOKING!

KNOWING HOW TO PREPARE YOUR own food is essential to maintaining a healthy, balanced diet. Cooking doesn't necessarily need to be super involved. There are plenty of quick and easy ways to prepare healthy—and delicious—food.

Plain and Simple Snacks

HERE ARE A FEW QUICK snack ideas.

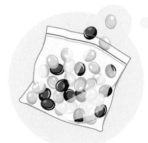

Frozen Grapes: Pop four handfuls of grapes in a plastic zip-top bag and put it in the freezer. Do it in the morning so you'll have a tasty snack when you get home from school.

Protein Sticks: Wrap a piece of lettuce around some string cheese or a slice of low-salt lunch meat and you'll be good to go.

Trail Mix: Mix a handful of raisins, dried cranberries, and unsalted nuts or granola in a zip-top bag. Carry the mix in your backpack for a quick snack in between classes.

Mexicana Relish: Mix a small container of plain, low-fat yogurt with three tablespoons of salsa. Spread on a few crackers and enjoy. The mix will stay fresh for five days in the fridge.

Frozen Yogsicles: Spray a clean, empty ice cube tray with cooking spray and spoon some of your favorite flavor yogurt into each section. Place a toothpick in the middle, allow to freeze, and— voilà!—you have yogsicles.

Fruit Smoothie: Combine one six-ounce container low-fat vanilla yogurt, half a banana,  two handfuls of strawberries (or banana or blueberries or any other fruit you like), and four ice cubes in a blender. Blend on high until the ice cubes are crushed. Pour your smoothie into a glass and enjoy!

HOW TO GO GROCERY SHOPPING

 GROCERY SHOPPING IS SOMETHING you might do along with one of your parents or an older brother or sister. They'll be really impressed if you make one or more of the following suggestions.

Don't go food shopping when you're hungry. When your stomach is growling, you may wind up buying food that looks good in the store but that you don't like at all when you get home. You are also more likely to fill your cart with unhealthy choices. So try to have a little snack before you hit the supermarket, or at least a glass of water to fill you up.

Shop along the outside aisles of the supermarket. Supermarkets usually have the healthiest and freshest foods there. The fruit, vegetable, dairy, and meat sections are on the outside, while snacks and less healthy processed foods are in the middle.

Always take a list to the store. You are more likely to stick to the fruits and vegetables and products you need and not buy unhealthy impulse items. Try to write the items in the order that you find them in the store. This will save you a lot of time—and you won't forget what you need!

Don't get hooked by sales and colorful displays at the end of aisles. Sure, those chocolate bars are a bargain and the chips look tasty, but just get one or the other, if you must—not all of them.

If you can't pronounce what's on the label, do you really want to eat it? The idea of learning to read a nutrition label is not so you get crazy about calories or fat or sugar. It's just so that you know what's in the food you eat *and* what's going into your body.

Sugar High

SUGAR TASTES GOOD, BUT IT DOESN'T give your body any nutrients—that's why calories from sugar are usually called "empty calories." If you eat too much sugar, you'll get an initial rush, then quickly crash and be left feeling tired and cranky. Too much of this sweet stuff isn't good for your smile, either, since sugar can cause tooth decay. And while you may have heard that brown sugar is healthier than white, it's a myth. Nutritionally there isn't much of a difference between them. And the brown color? That's created from molasses. There is such a thing as healthy sugar, though, such as that found in fruits. The key word here is "natural."

WATER WORKS!

WATER IS THE ESSENTIAL building block of all life. Every one of your cells has water in it. Your job is to drink H_2O (the chemical term for water) to keep all systems afloat! Here are a few of the good things water does:

- It gives your skin a beautiful glow and helps fight acne.

- It keeps the blood flowing in your system.

- It helps you maintain a healthy weight.

- It replenishes body fluids lost from normal sweating, urinating, and exercising.

- It helps you get rid of any toxins in your system.

The rule that you should drink six to eight (eight-ounce) glasses of water a day is a general guideline to go by, but don't wait until your throat is parched to have your first sip. The best way to stay hydrated is to drink small amounts of water throughout the day. With all the stylish and eco-friendly water bottles on the market, you have no excuse not to drink up!

You lose water through sweat and urination. When you exercise heavily or it's really hot out, drink more than normal to make sure you replace fluids you lose. And did you know that you lose a glass of water while you sleep? When you wake up each morning, drink an eight-ounce glass of water and you'll start the day completely hydrated.

Lots of foods that you already eat have water in them—lettuce, celery, and juicy fruits such as peaches and watermelon are just a few of many examples. A normal diet has about four cups of water in it, which means that by eating you are halfway to getting your daily quota.

You don't need to drink plain water to get enough H_2O. And if you don't like plain water, add a squeeze of fresh lemon or orange for some added—healthy—flavor! But any liquid you drink—such as juice, milk, or tea—has water in it and will help you get to your necessary total.

THE NO-FAD ZONE

EATING HEALTHY AND FEELING SAT-
isfied after a meal is not a fad. It's the best
way to enjoy food. Here are some simple tips
that will hold up in the long run:

Never let yourself get too hungry. Don't skip meals
(especially breakfast) or snacks. This is the most important habit you can form for a healthy, happy lifestyle.
Try not to miss an opportunity to eat something healthy,
since food is delicious and fuels your active day. Plus,
when you miss a meal, your body craves sugar and fat—
the things that are not good for you—and that's when
people tend to overeat.

Chew your food thoroughly. This will not only help you
feel more full and eat less, but it will also allow you to
enjoy every flavorful bite of your meal. Many of us tend

to gulp our meals down, which can leave us feeling hungry and unsatisfied.

Wait five minutes after eating a portion to see if you're still hungry before taking another helping. Give yourself some time to let the feeling of being satisfied set in. If the portions at a restaurant are too big, don't feel you have to finish it all. You can take the rest of the food home in a doggie bag and enjoy that delicious meal again the next day!

Sometimes when you think you're hungry, you're really thirsty—your body needs water. So if your stomach is grumbling and you haven't skipped a meal or snack, take a drink before you eat to see if you are actually hungry.

Eat food prepared at home whenever you can. Diners, delis, restaurants, and fast-food places add a lot of extra fat, sugar, and salt to make their food taste good. And they often fry their food. When food is prepared at home, you know exactly what's in it. It's also really fun to experiment with cooking. When you get good enough at it, you'll be able to make exactly what you want to eat.

Choose low-fat dairy products and lean proteins when you can. Low-fat milk or lean proteins such as chicken or pork are tasty and good for you! Many adults eat fat-free foods, but as a growing young person, low-fat is fine for you.

GOING TOO FAR

T'S FINE TO BE INTERESTED IN NUTRItion and keeping your weight at a healthy number. However, if you or a friend become too worried about eating and begin to have negative feelings about your body, you may be headed toward an eating disorder. This is when you have problems around food that can harm your mental and physical health. If you have any of these symptoms, please talk with a parent, guidance counselor, school nutritionist or nurse, or a family friend. They can help you find out more information from one of the many organizations that help tweens and teens overcome this condition. Eating disorders are serious but treatable if you get help.

Signs of a possible eating disorder:

- Intense fear of getting fat

- Extreme preoccupation with your body shape and weight

- Feeling fat even if you have lost a lot of weight

- Frequent dieting

- Out-of-control eating, even until feeling sick, followed by throwing up the food

YOU ARE WHAT YOU EAT

N THIS CHAPTER WE'VE LEARNED ABOUT food—what to go for and what to avoid. Of course, there's more to the story. For now, try eating in moderation—not too much and not too little. Have you heard the expression, "Listen to your body"? If you eat a meal and feel energetic, you've eaten healthfully. If any food makes you sleepy or if you have difficulty concentrating, take another look at what you've eaten. The way you feel is very much up to you!

chapter 3
SLEEP MATTERS

THE A TO ZZZZZZs OF SLEEP

SLEEP DOESN'T GET A LOT OF SPACE in fashion magazines—you never read about celebrities' sleep habits. That's okay, but what you've got to know is that sleep is really important to your health and beauty. In fact, each of us sleeps about one-third of our lives! It's more important than beauty products and makeup will ever be. You know that if you don't get a good night's sleep, you simply won't function well the next day. And if that doesn't convince you to turn in early, you stand the chance of getting dark circles under your eyes, your skin may lose its glow, or a pimple could pop up. In this chapter, we'll shed some light on what happens during those nighttime hours so you can really appreciate the magic of sleep.

What Is Sleep?

THERE ARE TWO TYPES OF SLEEP: REM (rapid eye movement) and NREM (nonrapid eye movement).

REM gets its name from the way the eyes dart back and forth while you are in this phase of sleep. It happens about ninety minutes after you fall asleep. REM is when most of your dreaming takes place and is when the brain is most active. See how much is happening while you slumber under the covers?

NREM takes up about 75 percent of your sleep time. It's the time when your blood pressure drops and your breathing becomes slower. Everything from your energy to your muscle tissue is restored during this process.

SLEEP AIDS

Trying to fall asleep can sometimes create stress for all of us. Here are a few things that can help with the process:

- **Have an active day.** Physical activity helps reduce stress and helps people feel more relaxed. Keep in mind that too much activity too close to bedtime can act as a stimulant. Start winding down a few hours before you go to sleep.
- **Sleep in a tech-free zone.** Shut everything down— that means OFF—when you go to sleep. No waiting

up all night for that IM or text. It will be there in the morning.

- Same time, same place. No falling asleep on the couch, then waking up and not being able to fall back to sleep. Go to sleep in your bedroom at the same time every night, and that way your body will begin to expect that sleep is coming on.

Why You Need Sleep

A LOT OF PEOPLE THINK THAT WHEN THEY are sleeping they aren't doing anything. That's so not true! Sleep time is one of the most important parts of your twenty-four-hour cycle. Your muscles might be relaxed, but your brain is still working. Think about all those dreams you have! While you are snoozing, your muscles are repairing themselves. Hormones that control growth and appetite are also released. A good night's sleep is the setup for a great day.

How Much Sleep You Need

BABIES NEED THE MOST SLEEP—UP TO eighteen hours a day! Older kids should aim for nine to eleven hours a night. So when your mom calls you lazy for lounging in bed, tell her you're getting the recommended daily dosage of sleep.

Sleep Schedule

YOU MIGHT BE A NIGHT OWL, AN EARLY BIRD, or something in between. Whatever your natural rhythm, having a regular time you wake up in the morning helps keep your brain and body in the right sleep-wake cycle. It's easier to fall asleep at night, and stay asleep, if you rise on schedule. It's actually good to stay on the same sleep schedule on the weekends as you do during the week, even though you could sleep later. To ease into sleep at night, forget about counting sheep. Come up with a nice, relaxing routine before you hit the hay.

It can include anything from taking a bath to medi-
tating to reading a book or listening to soft music. Just
avoid anything that stresses you out or gets your brain
buzzing—like IMing or television.

DREAM CATCHER

DREAMS ARE VERY MYSTERIOUS
ways our minds continue to work while
we're asleep. Dreams give us time to
review the events of a busy day and even help us figure out any problems that might be bothering us. Have
you ever heard someone say, "I'll sleep on it" or "I'll
think about it in the morning"? What they are really
saying is that they need time to think about something,
and some of that thinking takes place while they are
asleep, too. Try it! If something is bothering you one day,
decide that you will work on it while you are asleep.

Chances are you will wake up feeling much better about the problem, and you might even have found the solution.

For thousands of years people have tried to make sense of what objects or events mean in their dreams. There is a whole science of dream interpretation. It's fun to read some of these dream books, but keep in mind that these are just guidelines to get you thinking about what a particular dream means to you. The same exact dream may also mean different things to you at different times.

Dreams are usually pleasant and fun, but they can also be about things you're afraid of. If you happen to have a nightmare, it's always a good idea to talk about it with a parent or someone you trust. That seems to make things a little better.

Even though dreams race through our heads for about two hours at night, we don't always remember them. Even a very detailed dream will fly out of our heads the second we wake up. A good way to remember your dreams is to keep a dream journal and write down everything you remember as soon as you wake up. All it takes is a notebook and pen that you keep near your bed. Soon you'll find your book filled with colorful and exciting dreams that will be fun to go back and read. Dreams are a great outlet to help us see how creative our minds can be. Who knows? Your dreams might lead you to write an exciting adventure story or even a fantasy novel.

To get started tracking your own dreams, use the dream journal.

Dream Journal

WRITE DOWN ANY DETAILS YOU CAN remember from your dream, then try to interpret what it means in the spaces below.

DREAM:

INTERPRETATION:

DREAM:

INTERPRETATION:

Quiz: A Quick Snooze

True or False?

❄   ❄   ❄

1. **Kids of all ages need the same amount of sleep.**

   T   F

2. **You can't make up for lost sleep on the weekends.**

   T   F

3. **Your brain is at rest while you sleep.**

   T   F

4. **It's easier to fall asleep if your room is nice and warm.**

   T   F

5. **Resting isn't the same thing as sleeping.**

   T   F

6. **Boredom causes sleepiness.**

   T   F

Answers: 1. True. They both need anywhere from nine to eleven hours of sleep a night. 2. True. Lost sleep builds up and can be hard to make up if the total lost sleep becomes too great. Sleep deprivation is the cause of a lot of problems, including obesity and bad moods. 3. False. Your body might be resting, but even in the deepest sleep your brain is active and at work. During REM sleep, it's busy dreaming! 4. False. Actually a cool, dark room is the best environment to bring on sleepiness. 5. True. Lying down with your eyes closed does not equal real sleep, which is made up of two distinct biological processes, REM and NREM. 6. False. While a boring class or movie seems to bring on drowsiness, they're not the real cause. Only a lack of sleep causes sleepiness. Boring stuff only reveals the fact that you haven't had enough z's.

TO NAP OR NOT TO NAP?

F YOU DON'T GET ENOUGH SLEEP, IT'S BAD news. You can be cranky, have trouble making decisions, or find it hard to concentrate in school. You may also lack energy to play sports or hang out with friends. Sometimes it's hard to get to bed on time with your busy schedule. That's why the nap was invented! While naps don't make up for a good night's sleep, they can help make sure you don't get too overtired. That's right, naps aren't just for babies.

Researchers have discovered that naps can boost creativity and alertness in the later hours of the afternoon, when you start to feel sluggish. In studies, a nap of sixty minutes has been shown to improve alertness for ten hours! But you don't have to take an hour-long nap. Even a ten-minute snooze during the day can help improve your mood.

The best time to nap depends on whether you are

an early bird or a night owl. If your natural rhythm is to get up around six a.m. and turn in before ten p.m., then the best time for you to nap is around one p.m. If you like to sleep until eight a.m. or later and would love to go to bed around midnight if your parents let you, then two thirty p.m. is your nap time. However, it's likely you'll be in school at these hours; these suggested times are for weekends or vacations.

Find a quiet, dark place where you can relax. Breathe in and out slowly to calm your body. Think about relaxing your muscles one body part at a time. Now relax your mind by thinking about a peaceful place such as the beach, the woods, or anywhere that makes you happy. You'll be asleep in no time.

While researchers studied sixty-minute naps, you should not sleep for more than forty-five minutes. Otherwise you will wake up groggy, a feeling that can last up to half an hour.

WHAT A SNORE

S NORING CAN BE EMBARRASSING— especially when it keeps your friends up during a sleepover. It's a common problem, about ninety million Americans are affected by noisy breathing during sleep. The snorting sounds of snoring may be funny, but it's serious when it disrupts a good night's sleep, for you or others.

The best way to prevent snoring is sleeping on your side with a pillow elevating your head. Talk to your parents about using nasal strips that you can buy in a pharmacy. And dentists can prescribe dental appliances that ease the airway if your snoring is really a problem.

NIGHTTIME 911

SOME PEOPLE ARE GREAT SLEEPERS. Some aren't. That's just a fact of life. If you're having trouble falling asleep or staying that way through the night, there might be a simple reason for whatever's keeping you up at night. Here are a few common sources of sleep problems and simple solutions.

Problem: Eating too close to bedtime. Eating right before bed will often make you uncomfortable.

Solution: Finish your last meal *at least* three hours before you go to sleep. Snacks count too! You should get in the habit of not eating anything in those last hours before you doze off.

Problem: Liquids too close to bedtime. If you gulp down a gallon of water before you go to bed, you'll definitely wake up needing to go to the bathroom.

Solution: It's great to hydrate with a glass of water before you hit the hay. Just don't drink like you're about to embark on a five-mile hike! If you avoid spicy or salty food at dinner, you'll be less thirsty in the evening.

Problem: Exercising too close to bedtime. Regular exercise is a great way to ensure a good night's sleep. However, exercising or playing sports makes your body temperature rise, and it can take up to six hours for you to cool down!

Solution: Finish any strenuous physical activity at least six hours before bed. The late afternoon is the best time to be active, as exercise will contribute to a sound sleep.

❋   ❋   ❋

SLEEP ON IT

THIS BOOK IS ABOUT HELPING YOUR unique beauty shine through so you feel amazing and so others can see how truly incredible you are. As you can see from this chapter, the time you spend sleeping is just as important as the time you spend wide awake. So every night, get into your favorite pj's or nightgown and . . . sweet dreams!

The Ultimate Fitness and Nutrition Challenge

Test your knowledge!

1. **What are some common household objects you can use to exercise?**

2. **How can you easily gauge your target heart rate?**

3. **What is processed food?**

4. **How much water should you drink every day?**

5. **Counting sheep is the best way to fall asleep.**

chapter 4
CONFIDENCE CLUB

YOUR LIFE IS AN AMAZING ADVEN-
ture. Right now everything is changing
so quickly for you. You might like different
activities than you did when you were a little kid. Maybe
you've changed schools or just have different friends
now. You are certainly growing, which means your body
is changing as well. All these things are exciting, but they
can be a little scary, too. You need to value who you are
to make the ups and downs of this time a smooth ride.
The amount you value yourself is your self-esteem. If you

believe that you can nail any activity you try and anyone who doesn't want to be your friend is crazy, then you have high self-esteem. If you think you're crummy in school, sports, and everything else in your life, then your self-esteem is low. Most people fall somewhere in between these two extremes. Wherever you land on this spectrum, you can always build your self-esteem. Let's find out how.

GIVE YOUR SELF-ESTEEM SOME STEAM!

 **S**ELF-ESTEEM IS IMPORTANT BECAUSE it affects everything you do. When you feel good about yourself and appreciated by others, it's easier to make friends, try new activities, and push yourself to be a better student in school. This is

different from being conceited. You don't need to pretend you're the greatest person in the world. That would be really phony. A healthy self-image actually comes from accepting who you are—just the way you are. Here are some ways to improve your self-esteem.

Let lots of people into your life. Camp counselors, teachers, relatives, classmates, and neighbors make up your support network. Don't forget friends who move away—pen pals are a terrific hobby. Keep the members of this network updated on what's going on in your life. Their opinions, love, and guidance will come in handy one day.

Be helpful. Whether it's carrying an elderly person's groceries across the street or showing a new student around the school, helping out feels great. Making a difference in someone else's life will definitely make one in your own.

Try new experiences. Are you a jock? Then give drama a try. At first it might be intimidating to experiment with a new activity, but soon enough you'll find you've developed a host of new talents, skills, and friends!

Don't try to be perfect. Everyone makes mistakes. It's normal to worry about making them, but they are really lessons in disguise. So don't let the fear of mistakes keep you from trying new things. When you learn how to ride a bike, every time you fall off you are teaching your body how to balance. If you keep getting back on the bike, eventually you can ride like the wind . . . or at least to your friend's house.

Believe in yourself. Have faith that you can accomplish the goals you set for yourself. Make a plan for what you want to achieve and stick to it. You might not always end up where you thought you would, but you'll be better for the journey.

Ask for help. There's nothing wrong with asking for help when you need it. If you are stuck on a math problem, ask your friend the math whiz to explain it to you. You can learn from everybody in your life, not just your teachers. Your friends and family are a rich resource, so use them!

BEAUTIFUL ATTITUDE

ODY IMAGE IS THE MENTAL PICture you have of your physical appearance. Does that sound confusing? Simply put, it's what you see when you look at yourself. Your body is changing, and you may feel uncomfortable or embarrassed about these new physical developments. You may also feel bad that your friends are developing and you're not. You have to remember everyone develops at a different pace. Remember, no matter your shape

or size, you are beautiful and there are things to love about yourself.

The Ten Commandments of a Better Body Image

1. Thou Shalt Not Criticize Thyself. When you concentrate on what you believe are your limitations or weaknesses, you give them a lot of energy. In turn, that gives them power. Take that energy and put it toward your assets. Start by writing down one thing you like about yourself every day.

2. Thou Shalt Not Spend So Much Time at the Mirror. It's fine to check yourself out (it's especially a good idea to look in the mirror to make sure your shirt's buttoned right). And if you love what you see, go ahead and keep gazing. But if staring at your reflection makes you self-conscious, quit it. You have more important things to do.

3. Thou Shalt Not Worry About What Thou Can't Change. There are some things you simply can't change, like the color of your eyes or your height. So lamenting the fact that you aren't taller, or that your feet are too big, is simply a waste of time. If what's bothering you *is* in your control—like getting in shape—then start working on your goal instead of obsessing.

4. Thou Shalt Surround Thyself with Supportive People. If you spend time with nice people who care about you and compliment you on areas that really matter, you will definitely feel better about everything—including your body.

5. Thou Shalt Wear Comfortable Clothes. A dress can be the hottest trend in the world, worn by celebrities on the red carpet. Still, if it makes you feel awkward, take it off. There are plenty of fun styles to try, so don't force yourself into clothes you don't like.

6. **Thou Shalt Exercise.** Moving your body relieves stress and helps you get physically stronger. Exercise isn't about losing weight, it's about being healthier. When you get in shape, you'll feel great.

7. **Thou Shalt Not Weigh Thyself More than Once a Week.** If your physician says your weight is healthy for your height and age, then believe the doctor and move on. Worrying about the number on the scale is not as important as maintaining a healthy lifestyle.

8. **Thou Shalt Look at Others the Way You Would Like Others to Look at You.** Don't be overly critical of people's appearances. That means you shouldn't make fun of people for being tall or short, or wearing last season's shirt. If you judge people by how they look on the outside, you may miss a lot of great stuff inside.

9. **Thou Shalt Not Compare Thyself to Others.** Your best friend might have beautiful gray eyes, while yours are a deep shade of brown. Everyone is unique, and your beauty is all your own. So size yourself up by your own set of measurements.

10. **Thou Shalt Respect Thy Body.** Eat well, exercise, and get enough sleep. If you treat your body like the precious instrument it is, it will allow you to make beautiful music throughout your life.

Mirror, Mirror, on the Wall

IF YOU STUDIED YOUR COMMANDMENTS, you already know it's important to limit the time you spend gazing into the looking glass. But staring at yourself in the mirror can be a tool for a better body image if you do it the right way. People think they need to change their body to feel good about themselves—not so. They need to change how they see themselves. By age thirteen, 53 percent of American girls are "unhappy with their bodies." This percentage grows to 78 percent by the time girls reach seventeen. But you can beat this statistic if you follow the better body commandments. Here's how:

1. When you look in the mirror and think something cricitcal, such as "My nose is too big," immediately make yourself find one thing you like. It could be as small as your pinkie nail or as big as your smile.

2. Once you find what you like about yourself, say it out loud into the mirror three times. Get louder each time you repeat the sentence.

3. Try to find new things you like about your body each time you look. Soon you'll have so many choices, you won't know which sentence to say first.

IMPROVISE!

MPROV, SHORT FOR "IMPROVISATION," IS A form of theater in which the actors don't read off a script or follow any form of stage direction. They just say and do whatever comes to mind. Improv isn't limited to actors, however. People in all walks of life use improv to become better public speakers and improve their confidence. Not only that, but improv is also a lot of fun. Grab a friend and give these popular exercises a try.

Freeze Tag

THIS EXERCISE IS ALL ABOUT BODY MOVEMENT. It works best with groups of people. Person A starts by miming an activity, say playing tennis. When someone calls "Freeze!" Person A comes to a complete stop. Person B starts miming a new activity based on the frozen position of Person A. Maybe Person B decides to be washing a window. Someone calls "Freeze!" and Person C jumps in, and the cycle continues.

Yes, And

fast. You and a friend have a conversation. The only rule is you have to start each sentence with "Yes, and." For example, you might say, "I like your backpack." Your friend responds, "Yes, and it's filled with money!" Then you respond, "Yes, and money is good for buying clothes." And so on. See how long you can keep it up without breaking into hysterics.

Photograph

THIS EXERCISE TEACHES YOU HOW TO WORK with a group. It starts with one person freezing in a position. One by one, others join in to make a photograph. When the last person joins in, the group decides what's happening in the photo and what each person is doing. Maybe it's a straightforward family photo, with mom, dad, son, daughter, and dog. Or it could be more abstract, like a photo of a forest or other scene from nature.

YOU CAN SOMETIMES BE YOUR OWN BEST FRIEND

FRIENDS CAN'T ALWAYS PLAY IN the park. Your mom can't always drive you to the mall and go shopping. Sometimes you find yourself alone—and that's okay. Alone time should be a great time. It's actually a gift. When you are alone, you can do whatever you want. Well, almost. Check out the alone time dos and don'ts to see if you're making the most of it!

Do!

- Go anyplace else you would go with a friend. Just because you're alone doesn't mean you can't enjoy activities you usually do with other people. The experience will be different, but you will still have fun.

- Pamper yourself. Get a pedicure or take a long bath.

- Take a long walk. Accompanied by your own thoughts, this is a terrific way to get some exercise and catch up with yourself.

Don't!

- Pitch a fit. Don't get angry with your family or friends who might have canceled plans with you.

- Plop on the couch for a TV marathon. Being alone isn't an excuse to zone out for countless hours.

- Dial yourself into a frenzy. You don't need to call

everyone on your cell phone to pass the time. Hang up that phone and start a conversation with one of the coolest people you know—you!

SPEAK UP!

YOU ARE SO PASSIONATE ABOUT SO many subjects. Why not share your passions with the world? There are many ways to express yourself—fashion, friends, schoolwork, and sports are just a few. Another wonderful way is straight talk. Sounds simple, right? Not always. You and your friends go to a movie, and everyone hates it except you! You loved it. Do you speak up and share your opinion, or do you keep it to yourself because you don't want to be different from the group?

Getting things off your chest is crucial to feeling good about yourself. Even if you are naturally shy, talking to others about your true emotions isn't important only for your self-esteem. It also helps build strong relationships with the people around you. You can practice what you want to say before you say it. That way, if you get nervous, which is totally normal, you will have already worked on your ideas.

It's also important to talk in class. You are smart, but you need to show that to your teacher and classmates. Nobody will know you have the answers if you keep them to yourself. If this doesn't come naturally to you, it will be pretty hard at first. But the more you do speak up, the easier it will get. Challenge yourself to speak in class or to someone new each day. It's time to get talking!

Talk Helps and Hurts

WHEN YOU TALK, YOU CAN'T SEE WORDS, but you can definitely feel them. Especially when they hurt. There's a saying, "Sticks and stones may break my bones, but words will never hurt me." Who said that?

Name-calling *does* hurt. When you're angry, you might be tempted to say mean things. But if you call someone stupid, fat, ugly, or any other kind of terrible word, it will stick with them, and you, for a long, long time. So beware of words. They are strong stuff.

Gossip is another land mine you should avoid. It can seem like fun to be part of a bunch huddled together, whispering secrets during recess. Think about how it would feel if you were the subject of the gossip being spread. Doesn't sound so great anymore, huh? Basically, if you wouldn't want it said about you, don't say it about others. Politely excuse yourself from the gossip group—you don't have to say why if you're embarrassed—and go do something more fun.

How to Ask for What You Want and Get It . . . Sometimes

LEARNING TO USE YOUR VOICE TO STAND UP for yourself is important to being happy. But even adults struggle with finding the courage to ask for what they want. It's totally understandable to feel jumpy inside when asking for a raise in your allowance or for a big favor from a friend. To make the conversation go a little smoother, try out the tips below. Whether or not you get what you asked for, going for what you want will make you feel better. Promise.

See Eye-to-Eye

Making eye contact is step number one. Looking someone in the eye is a big sign that you are confident and believe in what you are saying. It's also a chance to make a real connection with the person you hope will give you what you want!

Smile

Oh yeah, that again. Smiling never hurts. Don't be fake, but a warm smile will put everyone in the discussion at ease.

Body Language

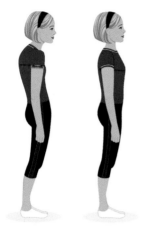

Your body says as much as your words. Even if you are really nervous as you approach the conversation, fake confidence by standing straight with your shoulders back. Don't hunch over, since it's a sign that you don't feel worthy of your request. And don't cross your arms, which looks like you are ready for a fight.

No Crybabies

Don't whine for what you want. You'll get a lot more sympathy for your cause if you simply state your wishes. And don't complain if things don't go your way. Instead, try to understand the other person's argument by listening. You might find a compromise, and you'll definitely be more convincing if you decide to ask again later.

Practice Makes Perfect

If you have something really hard to ask, you might want to first write down your thoughts on a piece of paper. What do you want to say? What are you trying to achieve? Once you have a clear idea, grab a friend or parent and practice what you want to say out loud. You might stutter or stammer at first, but the more you repeat your request, the easier it will become to say it straight.

Never Say You're Sorry

Ever heard someone say, "I'm sorry, but can I ask you a question?" You don't need to apologize. Just ask! It's perfectly fine wherever you are—at home, at school, or with your friends. So go ahead and ask away.

LET'S MAKE A DEAL

NEGOTIATING ISN'T JUST SOME-thing your mom and dad do when they want a raise at work. You need to learn to put this important tool to work in your life at home and school! Negotiating is a process where two different people talk until they come to an agreement where you both feel like you won. Let's not waste another second! Here are some tips to help you negotiate.

1. **Know what you want.** This might sound simple, but Amy says, "This is the hardest part of the process, because you really have to think about what would make you happy." Do you really want that new shirt? Or if you consider the situation, do you find yourself asking for one item every month? Maybe this means you really want a raise in your allowance so you can manage how

you spend your money. Make sure you have your true end goal in sight.

2. Think very hard about what the other person wants. This isn't easy either. You need to get inside the brain of the person you are negotiating with—what could you give them in return? "You'll be in a position of power if you can anticipate what they are going to want," Amy explains. In the example of your raise in allowance, perhaps you know that your parents really want you to babysit your little sister. That's a start.

3. Know what you are willing to give up. "And always ask for more than you want," Amy counsels. Here's where you seal the deal: So you want a raise in your allowance and know your parents want you to babysit. You would be willing to babysit every other week for that extra cash, so you offer to babysit once a month. They say, "No way!" and ask you to sit for your sister once a

week. You meet them in the middle and agree to every other week. Your original goal! You get your money, your parents get a sitter, and your sister has an awesome role model. Like Amy says, everybody wins.

FAMILY AFFAIR

OOD COMMUNICATION STARTS at home, and it can start with you! Take a leadership role by organizing monthly meetings with your family to keep talk open, honest, and current.

Get it on the calendar: The first step, and the hardest for most families, is finding a date and time when everyone can meet. Once you find one that works for

everyone, mark it on a wall calendar. Make the meeting place around the dinner table, or any space where the entire gang will feel comfortable.

Listen up: The family meeting isn't a solo performance. Let other people finish what they are saying without interrupting. Be interested in what others are talking about. It's especially nice to ask about events that have happened, like how your mom's big meeting went or if your brother aced his math exam. Your attention means a lot to everyone, even your folks!

Grown-up behavior: If you are mature enough to start these meetings, then you have to be mature enough to participate in a grown-up way. Your sister might say something hurtful—that can happen when people are speaking about deep and true feelings. When that happens—and it will if everyone is honest—don't immediately react. That means don't scream, throw chairs, or have a fit, even though you probably feel like you want to. Take a deep breath, or three, and hear your family member out. Then it will be your turn to vent. And it may sound silly, but your posture can affect the way your family reacts to what you have to say. Sit up straight, and you'll see how much easier it is to speak with confidence—and get everyone to listen!

NO REJECTS ALLOWED

T FEELS TERRIBLE TO HEAR THE WORD "no." It stinks when you're not invited to a party. Your stomach takes a tumble when you learn you didn't make the team. Unless you are living in a cave, rejection is an ordinary part of life. No one is saying it's easy to take. But if you are going to take risks, you have to be ready for a little rejection.

The key to dealing with rejection is not to take it personally. What? You're thinking, "But it *is* personal."

If you don't get picked for a part in the school play or a guy you like asks someone else to the school dance, it's not about you. A lot goes into any decision, and many things are out of your control. Maybe that boy doesn't know you like him. Maybe the drama teacher gave the part to someone who has helped out with the props. Maybe neither the play nor the boy is right for you. What *is* in your control is your attitude. You can find another boy, audition for another play. Winners try and try again.

Quiz: Famous Rejects

Guess which famous people faced a lot of REJECTION before they hit it big? Three of the following people experienced serious obstacles before they succeeded in their chosen fields. Circle three names and see if you are right.

❄   ❄   ❄

J. K. Rowling

Albert Einstein

Mozart

Madonna

Michael Jordan

Answer: The first of the Harry Potter books—the fastest-selling series of all time—was rejected by twelve publishers before it finally made it to print! Potter fans all over the world are lucky that author J. K. Rowling refused to give up on her dreams. Michael Jordan was cut from his high school basketball team in his sophomore year, but he didn't give up—he practiced even more, tried out again the next year, and went on to become one of the greatest NBA players and athletes of all time. One of the greatest minds of the twentieth century, Albert Einstein failed his first college entrance exam. He figured out the theory of relativity, but he flunked a test thousands could pass. Luckily, he was smart enough to take it again.

CRITICAL APPROACH

T'S NOT EASY TO TAKE CRITICISM. NOBODY likes to hear how they could have written a school assignment more clearly or could have done a better job making their bed. But none of us is perfect, so getting a little criticism is a way to improve. It's like turning lemons into lemonade. There are a few ways to make the giving and getting of advice a lot easier to take.

The Three Be's of Offering Criticism

1. Be nice. For any conversation where you want to offer some criticism, start with something positive. If your best friend is making you sad because she's been spending more time with new friends than with you, tell her how much you love her and miss hanging out with her.

Remind her of some fun times you've had together. That will work a lot better than if you accuse her of being a jerk for ignoring you.

2. **Be upbeat.** Don't scold, nag, or whine. When you have a good attitude, acting warm and open, you will put the other person at ease. Smile and look directly at the person you are talking to.

3. **Be part of the solution.** Offer some practical ways to fix the issue. Don't put it all on the other person. You should make an effort as well. For that friend who has grown apart, you could suggest a few fun and new activities to do that would mean spending time together in a great way.

The Three Don'ts for Getting Criticism

1. **Don't protest.** If someone you care about has taken the trouble to give you feedback, you should assume

there is truth to what they are saying. Don't fight or try to deny it. If someone had the courage to confront you, listen and see if you can understand what she's talking about.

2. **Don't be closed-minded.** You aren't always going to agree with someone else's ideas. In the end, you have to be happy with your beliefs and behavior. But let's say a teammate tells you that you hog the soccer ball on the field, and you don't believe her. Try gently asking some other teammates to find out what they think. If a few agree, it's safe to say you're probably a ball hog.

3. **Don't get stuck in your ways.** You are great just the way you are, but that doesn't mean you can't learn new skills and insights. Criticism is a chance to do things differently. Take that chance and find out where trying something different takes you.

chapter 5
CALM, COOL, AND COLLECTED

T'S A SUPER-EXCITING TIME TO BE A KID. When your parents were young, there weren't nearly as many things to do. But kids today are also under a lot more pressure. Jam-packed schedules, technology overload, and never-ending homework are just a few of the culprits. Because life is so hectic, you need to learn how to unwind. If you don't take time to recharge, you'll run your body ragged. Any doctor will tell you that stressed-out people get sick a lot more than those who can relax. Of course, there's a right way and a wrong way to take a load off. Watching TV might sound relaxing, but it's not nearly as invigorating as reading a great book.

Quiz: Stress Test

Do you bite your fingernails all the time? Or do you barely break a sweat when your teacher hands out a pop quiz? Take this quiz to see how stressed out you are.

❄   ❄   ❄

1. **When you walk into a school dance, the first thing you do is:**

   A. race to the bathroom to triple-check that you don't have any spinach in your teeth (1 point)

   B. hang on the sidelines with your friends, watching the action (2 points)

   C. dance like crazy with your best buds in the middle of the floor (3 points)

2. **You have trouble falling asleep at night:**

   A. never (3 points)

   B. once in a while (2 points)

   C. a lot (1 point)

3. **At a restaurant where the menu is a mile long, you:**

   A. ask the waiter about the specials (2 points)

   B. pick your favorite standby dish (3 points)

   C. read the menu about fifty times and then make

   your mom choose for you (1 point)

4. **The color that best goes with your personality is:**

   A. bright red (1 point)

   B. sky blue (3 points)

   C. pale pink (2 points)

5. **When faced with a Saturday completely free of**

activities and obligations, you:

A. find a comfy, quiet corner of the house to read, draw, listen to music, or do whatever you feel like (2 points)

B. get back in bed (3 points)

C. make a list of all the chores, homework, and plans you have (1 point)

6. **Standing in front of the ocean, you are:**

A. lulled by the lapping waves (2 points)

B. worried about drowning (1 point)

C. concerned with your tan (3 points)

7. **When your teacher hands you a test, you:**

A. hyperventilate (1 point)

B. grab your pencil and get to work (2 points)

C. space out and think about what you'll eat for lunch (3 points)

8. **If you were in a completely white room with no windows, you would:**

   A. zone out (3 points)

   B. redecorate in your head (2 points)

   C. start beating your fists against the door (1 point)

9. **Your nighttime routine includes:**

   A. a long bath and a good book (3 points)

   B. finishing up a homework assignment in bed (1 point)

   C. sacking out in front of the TV (2 points)

10. **If you were an animal, you would be:**

   A. a cat (3 points)

   B. a dog (2 points)

   C. a squirrel (1 point)

If you scored . . .

10–17 points:

IT'S TIME FOR YOU TO TAKE A VACATION. YOUR stress level is off the charts! You have so much going on that at times it can get overwhelming. That's totally understandable, but you have to give yourself a break every now and then. Take some deep breaths and remember, tomorrow is another day. So take a moment to relax. Then you can go back to your hectic lifestyle.

18–24 points:

ON THE FIRST DAY OF SCHOOL, YOU GET A FEW jitters. Same with diving off the high board. Generally speaking, though, your stomach is not a hospitable environment for butterflies. When you do get stressed out, rely on simple coping techniques such as stretching, taking a hot bath, or drinking some warm milk. They might sound corny or old-fashioned, but they work!

25-30 points:

IF YOU WERE ANY CALMER, YOU MIGHT NOT HAVE a pulse. Nothing gets you nervous. It's just your nature—you've been this way since you were a baby. You're lucky in a lot of ways. Nerves never keep you from trying a new activity or meeting new friends. But sometimes your cool attitude can border on laziness. Perhaps if you were a little more worried about that test, you would study harder. You would benefit from making a list of things that need to get done—that way you won't get so relaxed you forget something important.

RELAX YOURSELF

STRESS IS AN UNAVOIDABLE PART of a busy and full life. School, family, and  friends all make demands on you. You wouldn't give up any of it for a second, but sometimes it's hard to juggle them all. When stress takes over, even the most fun activity can feel like a drag. That's why relaxation and calm shouldn't be reserved for vacations alone. Try these de-stressing tips for two weeks. Your schedule will still be hectic, but you'll feel a lot more peaceful.

Get a Massage

A MASSAGE IS A WONDERFUL WAY TO smooth out those knots. But you don't have to pay for an expensive treatment at a spa. Even a fifteen-minute massage will work wonders. Create a massage circle with friends, where everyone who participates gives a massage while getting one. You can also take a minute out

of your day to massage the fleshy spot in your palm with your other hand or rub your shoulders, a place that often tightens up when things get tense. Every little bit helps.

Breathe

THE FOUNDATION OF YOGA, THOUGHT TO be the exercise of relaxation, focuses on how you breathe. When you feel stressed, take a second to see if you're holding your breath; sometimes we do that without realizing it. Practice a breathing technique: Make your stomach go in and out with each breath. When you're feeling frustrated or stressed, try some special breathing—do a set of five in and out breaths, take a five-count break, and try another set.

Drink Tea

STUDIES HAVE SHOWN THAT DRINKING TEA can lower levels of stress hormones. If you do drink tea, make sure it's decaffeinated, since caffeine is *not* relaxing. Try an herbal tea—chamomile and mint are good choices. Really, sipping any hot beverage—warm milk or hot cocoa included—is a surefire way to cool down.

Enjoy Simple Pleasures

THE IDEA OF LOUNGING IN FRONT OF THE TV or chatting online with friends seems super relaxing,

but watching the boob tube or logging on actually puts all your senses through their paces. Try single-sensory forms of entertainment, like reading, listening to the radio, or even doing a puzzle like Sudoku, when you're feeling keyed up. If you play a musical instrument, playing your favorite tunes is also pleasurable.

Plant a Flower

GROWING ANY KIND OF PLANT OR VEGETABLE

is a great way to mellow out. Tending to a window box or vegetable garden can lower your heart rate and improve your mood.

Laugh

YOU ALREADY KNOW HOW great it is to laugh. A serious fit of giggles relaxes your whole mind and body. That's because laughter releases something called endorphins, which are chemicals produced by the brain that make you feel good. So crack jokes with your friends, have fun, and get ready to feel fantastic.

THE POWER OF NO

YOU OFFERED TO MAKE DECORA-tions for your best friend's birthday party, help your little brother with his homework, and walk your neighbor's cute new puppy. You are way overextended and have no idea how or if you'll get it all done. Does this situation sound familiar? You make so many plans and accept so many invitations that you either wind up canceling at the last minute or you don't do as good a job as you would like. Either way the result is that your stress level goes through the roof and activities you love become a burden.

It's sometimes hard to say no, especially to people you love. You might worry that a friend won't continue to be your friend if you tell her you can't go to the movies or the mall. But that's not true. Nobody wants to hang out with you because you say yes all the time. In fact, you will get respect for saying no when you need to, especially if you say it in a nice way. When you set priorities, you can spend more time on things you really love to do. Who can say no to that?

BABY STEPS

T'S VERY COMMON TO FEEL ANXIOUS AND overwhelmed by big projects, whether it's a long book report for school or packing for camp. Big projects come with big rewards, so it's important to learn how to manage them. The best way to get rid of stress is to break a large, complicated task down into smaller, easier steps—otherwise known as baby steps!

Sample Project: Organize Your Closet

THE GOAL IS TO TAME A MESSY MONSTER of a closet into a clean and neat one.

Baby Step 1: Take all the clothes out of your closet.

Baby Step 2: Sort the clothes into two piles, one to keep and one to give away.

Baby Step 3: Sort the "keep" pile into different types of clothes, such as shirts, pants, and skirts.

Baby Step 4: Remove clothes that need cleaning or mending.

Baby Step 5: Fold or hang all shirts neatly and put away in the closet.

Baby Step 6: Hang up all pants and skirts.

Baby Step 7: Lie on your bed and admire your hard work and neat closet!

Real-Life Projects

TAKE YOUR PROJECT AND COME UP WITH THE very first step—that's Baby Step 1. Then write the steps that follow from there. Aim to break it down into at least five steps. Use a pencil, because as you complete each step, the next steps may change. If you don't know what step one should be, just start anywhere and you can put them in order when you finish your list. Just start!

Project Name:

BABY STEP 1:

BABY STEP 2:

BABY STEP 3:

BABY STEP 4:

BABY STEP 5:

WORK IT OUT

EXERCISING BENEFITS YOUR BODY in many ways. It strengthens your muscles, lowers your blood pressure, and reduces the risk of diseases such as diabetes. It also makes your skin glow!

The amazing thing about working out is that it also does wonders for your brain. Kids who exercise do better in school and have lower rates of anxiety. There are some chemical reasons for this. Remember those endorphins that produce feelings of well-being that we talked about earlier? Well, they are released when you do anything strenuous, like running really far or really fast.

There are also some practical reasons physical activity affects your mood. It tires you out so that you sleep better, and enough sleep is essential for a bright attitude. You can energize your self-esteem when you accomplish your goals. So skateboard to school, skip rope, or jump on your Wii Fit. Your brain will thank you.

YOGA TIME

YOGA IS ONE TYPE OF EXERCISE that's especially good for relaxing. An ancient tradition that fits perfectly in the fast-paced modern world, it combines meditation with physical exercise for a full mind/body workout. You might be having the most stressed-out day of your entire life, but after an hour on the yoga mat, you'll feel balanced and recharged again.

More than sixteen million Americans practice yoga, so you don't have to feel intimidated about trying it. The trick is figuring out which kind of yoga is right for you. The following chart describes the main options, from easiest to most difficult.

Type of Yoga	How Does It Work?
Hatha	This slower-paced class covers basic yoga techniques, simple breathing, and light meditation.
Kundalini	This form of yoga combines lots of chanting with basic yoga poses.
Vinyasa	This yoga involves many different poses, as well as breathing exercises chosen by your instructor.
Iyengar	The focus is on alignment. Students hold precise poses with the help of props; for example, straps and wooden blocks.
Ashtanga	This is one of the most chaellenging. Each class includes twenty-five poses or more.
Bikram	This yoga includes more than twenty-five poses, but this is performed in a very heated room.

How Hard Is It?

LOW IMPACT, which makes this the perfect place for beginners.

. . . .

LOW IMPACT. Not as tough as most yogas
(provided you're comfortable chanting in front of strangers!).

. . . .

IT DEPENDS on the instructor, so if it's your first time,
look for a class designed for beginners.

. . . .

MEDIUM. Holding perfectly still for thirty seconds
or longer is a challenge in the beginning.

. . . .

HIGH. Even beginner classes can be difficult in this
form of yoga, so be prepared for a workout.

. . . .

EXTREMELY HIGH. This is for hardcore yogis who are super fit
(and have clearance from their doctors to work out in extreme heat).

MIND OVER MATTER

N *PETER PAN,* WHEN PETER IS TEACHING Wendy to fly, he tells her to "think lovely thoughts." Then, guess what? She starts to fly. That's what you call the power of positive thinking. Positive thinking is such a strong force that it can make real changes. It might not happen overnight, but when you think lovely thoughts, amazing things occur.

Let's get started with those lovely thoughts right away. Take the negative sentences below and turn them around into positive statements.

I don't like my body. I love my body. My body is amazing. It gets me around to all my favorite activities and is loyal, hardly ever letting me down by getting sick.

I'm not pretty. I am beautiful. My beauty starts inside me and shines through every day.

142

Real-Life Projects

NOW YOU TRY! Turn these negatives around with your own lovely thoughts and experience the power of positive thinking.

I'M NOT ATHLETIC.

I'M NOT SMART.

I'M NOT IMPORTANT.

BLUES BUSTERS

EVERYONE GETS DOWN IN THE dumps sometimes, but you don't have to stay there for long. Below is a very different kind of to-do list from your usual notebook filled with chores or homework assignments. This is a file of activities that will snap you out of that bad mood. So next time you find yourself singing the blues, grab this list, and before you know it, you'll be rocking out.

☐ **Talk to a family member:** This is probably the best blues blaster around. No one knows you better than your family. Talking makes you feel better, and you usually realize that your problem isn't as big as you thought it was.

☐ **Get crafty:** Nothing absorbs bad vibes like a good craft project. Make a friendship bracelet or tie-dye a shirt. Turn your photos into a colorful scrapbook. Working with your hands and getting lost in the small details will take you far away from your troubles. Plus, you'll have something really cool when you're done.

☐ Cook up a storm: Bake your favorite treat, whether that's cupcakes or oatmeal cookies. The delicious smell of the ingredients will elevate your mood, and the finished creation will be a comforting reward for your efforts. Just be sure to make enough for others.

☐ Create a cool playlist: Music can transport you to any place or time. Pick songs that remind you of great summer trips or memorable moments with your best pals. Once you have your playlist, have a dance party for one in your bedroom or sit somewhere pretty, like your backyard, while listening to your iPod.

☐ **Smile while walking down the hallway in school:**
This might seem silly and will probably make you
feel nervous at first. But when you smile first, people
instinctively smile back. The energy between two
smiles is electric! Once you release a few smiles, you'll
be addicted.

☐ **Stop texting and turn off your IM:** Those are both
great ways to stay in touch with friends, but sometimes
you need to see the people you love face-to-face. Get
out of your house and make human contact! There's
nothing like it.

Quiz: What's Your State of Mind?

Are you the one your friends always turn to when times are tough? Do you cheer the loudest at every activity? Or are you more skeptical and need a lot of encouragement before you'll dive into a situation?

1. **Did you smile more than frown today?**

   A. yes

   B. no

2. **When a new club starts up at school, are you one of the first people to join?**

   A. yes

   B. no

3. Does it take you a long time to accept a new person as a friend?

    A. yes

    B. no

4. When someone makes you mad or upset, do you have a hard time forgiving her?

    A. yes

    B. no

5. If something doesn't go your way, like a pop quiz in school, does it ruin your mood for the rest of the day?

    A. yes

    B. no

Answer Key

MOSTLY As: You're the kind of person who can find the bright side on even the rainiest of days. You have friends from all different groups at school and could find fun in an empty paper bag. Sometimes that can be hard—especially when everyone is always looking to you to be the life of the party—but your great attitude will take you far.

MOSTLY Bs: You tend to think about things before you act, and sometimes that leads to brooding. Your sensitive nature can quickly turn to negative thoughts, since you have a lot on your mind. It's wonderful that you contemplate your actions so seriously, but don't let them take over. You are allowed to take a few chances and make some mistakes.

RELATIONSHIPS MATTER

THERE IS AN AFRICAN PROVERB: IT takes a whole village to raise a child. That means a kid needs more than just a mom or dad while growing up—and that's not just in Africa! The more adults you have in your life, the easier it is to find help with any difficulties you may have and to share all your triumphs.

Relationships with grandparents, cousins, uncles, teachers, and other grown-ups can expand your perspective, not only of your situation but also on the whole wide world. Here's a fun experiment: Ask a few different adults you know the same question—it can be anything on your mind. What's the definition of a good friend? Or how did you figure out what kind of job you wanted? Compare the answers you get. You'll be surprised at the range of opinions, and you can probably learn something from all of them.

chapter 6
CARING FOR YOURSELF
AS WELL AS OTHERS

T'S IMPORTANT TO ALWAYS LOOK OUT

for yourself, but you have to remember to look out for

others, too. Never before have people been more

connected—thanks to cell phones, social networking

pages, and other technologies that keep us plugged

into one another at all times. That can be great when

you want to reach your mom in a flash so she can pick

you up from a sleepover, but it can also be not so great

when you're having a fight with your BFF and you see

she's IMing with another girl in your class instead of you.

To be happy and successful in life, you need to be able to manage your relationships with all the people in your social network, whether they're friends, family, or people in the community you live in. This means giving as much as you receive. It means caring as much as you're cared for. It means treating others as you would like to be treated. The best thing about this is that when you do good, you'll feel good inside.

FRENEMIES

YOU MAY LOVE YOUR FRIENDS AS IF they were your family. They can sometimes make you laugh harder than you thought possible, but they can also make you cry. When you are in a superclose relationship, you and your friend's actions mean a lot to each other. That's why friendship can be beautiful *and* it can be bumpy. Here are a few common situations you may have with pals and how to deal with them.

The Faraway Friend: You and a friend talk on the phone every day, sometimes for hours before you go to bed. You walk to school together and swap clothes. It's like you're practically joined at the hip. And then suddenly—you're not. That same friend is drifting away, not answering your e-mails and getting off the phone quickly. You know you didn't do anything to offend her, so what gives? And how can you get her back?

The solution: Sometimes friends fall out of touch for no good reason. Don't attack the person by e-mail or letter, since that will probably make her retreat even more. The best method is a low-key one. Hang back from her life for a while and occasionally extend an invitation to the movies or some other event you both enjoy. You won't come off as too eager, but she'll know you are there for her.

The Copycat: You decide to paint a sunset in art class, and your friend next to you does the same. While planning a karaoke birthday, you receive an invitation to your friend's sing-along bash. On the first day of school, you run into your twin wearing—that's right—the exact same dress. Coincidence, or a case of the copycats?

The solution: It's a drag, but just know that imitation is the highest form of flattery. If a friend cribs your style or joins your activity, try to see it as a good thing. Hey, you've got great taste. If the imitation becomes a nuisance, consider taking your friend aside and talking to her. In a gentle way, say you love that she appreciates your choices but that you want to keep your clothes, projects, or plans unique. Then offer to pick out an outfit that will look great on just her.

The Blabbermouth: Some friends aren't great at keeping secrets. In fact, they are terrible at it. Anything you tell them spreads faster than wildfire. Is someone really a friend if you can't trust her with confidential information?

The solution: Secrets are overrated. If someone is a good friend in every way other than keeping her mouth shut, chances are that's a friend worth having. Just don't tell her anything you don't want everyone to know.

DEALING WITH BULLIES

There's at least one at every school. Ugh. Bullies. Most kids get bullied at some point in their lives. For anyone who has been pushed, teased, or taunted, you know that it can make you feel scared, angry, and embarrassed. The fear of confronting a bully can get so bad that some kids get physically sick over the situation. If you're being bullied, it's important to know that you aren't alone and that you can do something about it.

Avoid the bully. No one is suggesting that you skip school or not go to a party just to avoid seeing someone. In fact, you should purposely *not* not go! Just know that you aren't a coward if you choose to take a longer path to lunch or hang out in the library during recess to steer clear of the person bothering you. Sometimes it's just plain smart.

Find a friend. There's safety in numbers. Keep a good friend close during lunch, recess, or on your way home. Some bullies will leave you alone if someone else is around. Offer to do the same for your friends if they get bullied.

Ignore the bully. When she starts her tease-fest, ignore it. Easier said than done, but bullies are looking to get a rise out of you. Pretend you can't hear what she's saying and leave the area immediately.

Put on a brave face. You may not feel brave, but if you act like you have courage, your feelings will follow.

Yelling "No!" is a good way to act like you're strong.

Tell an adult. This is very important. Don't worry that kids will think you're a tattletale. Chances are, other kids are also being bullied. Teachers and parents need to know if someone is threatening you. It's their job to protect you, so let them do it!

GIVING BACK

HELPING PEOPLE LESS FORTUNATE than you and making the world better are essential components to a happy life. It's true! Being a well-rounded person means that charity work has a place next to hanging out with friends and enjoying hobbies. You'll be surprised how great it feels to focus on the needs of others. It offers a sense of satisfaction you can't find any other way. Don't worry—you don't have to raise a half million dollars and design a purse to give back! There are plenty of easier ways to make a difference. Here are a few of Ali's favorite ideas.

DONATE USED CLOTHES AND TOYS. This is one of Ali's favorite activities. Every year on her birthday, she collects clothes and objects she no longer uses and brings them to a local shelter where they accept donations. Talk to your parents about a local organization that will accept used items and show them your donations before you give anything away.

BRIGHTEN AN ELDERLY PERSON'S DAY. Singing, dancing, cracking jokes—whatever your talent is, take it to a nursing home. Many assisted living facilities have programs where young people can visit their residents. Ask your parents to help you locate a home near you.

BAKE FOR BUCKS. Choose a charity with your

parents and then hold a bake sale outside your house to raise money for it. If you are a terrible cook, substitute lemonade.

GIVE ENCOURAGEMENT. Sending a note to a friend who is sick or going through a hard time can make a world of difference and only takes five minutes.

CARRY GROCERIES. When you walk out of the store, look for someone who needs help with their groceries. This could be an older person or a mom with young kids. Politely offer to carry the bags to their car (make sure an adult you know is supervising). And don't worry if they don't take you up on it. It's the offer that counts.

RECYCLE. The environment needs all the help it can get. Learn about the recycling laws in your neighborhood and follow them. Also reduce the waste you produce by drinking water from reusable bottles and thinking twice before you print anything out from your computer.

JOIN A GROUP DOING GOOD DEEDS. Find out about charitable activities at your school, church, or any organization you belong to, and join up. You will do good deeds and make new friends!

EXPRESS YOURSELF

THERE IS SO MUCH TO PONDER IN life. You've got a lot going on, and every day new changes seem to crop up. There's no better way to keep stock of your thoughts and feelings than keeping a journal. Recording your experiences in a journal helps you sort out your emotions and learn more about the fantastic person you are.

Your diary doesn't have to be a fancy book with

a lock and key. Journals come in all shapes and sizes. You can keep one on index cards, or on the computer. You don't even have to write at all; you can record your thoughts on a digital tape recorder instead. The challenge is setting aside a little time, ideally every day, to get your thoughts out. It's helpful if you try to write in your diary around the same time every day. It could be morning, noon, or night—whatever works best for you.

Keeping a journal allows you to clear your mind. It's also a wonderful record of your life that you will find fascinating to read over and over as the years go by.

My Journal

WRITE DOWN YOUR THOUGHTS ABOUT THESE topics and get into the habit of keeping a journal.

LIFE GOALS:

WHAT I LIKE ABOUT ME:

ROLE MODELS:

BOOKS I'VE READ:

The Ultimate Self-Esteem Challenge

Test your knowledge!

❄   ❄   ❄

1. **What should you do if you're being bullied?**

2. **What do cooking, doing crafts, talking to a family member, making a playlist, and smiling have in common?**

3. **What body part is essential in having a good body image?**

4. What's the first step of any negotiation?

5. What's the best way to give back?

Answers: 1. The most important thing you can do is tell an adult you trust, like a parent or teacher. It's hard to talk about it, but an adult can help you figure out a solution to your problem. 2. These are all good ways to pick yourself up when you are feeling low. They help you get your mind off any worries you might have. 3. Your brain! Your attitude and perspective are what determine whether or not you love and accept your body. 4. You have to know what you want before you negotiate for it. This is often the hardest part of the process! 5. Make sure whatever you choose is something you already love to do. If you love to work in the garden, plant trees at a local park. If you love to play the piano, tickle the ivories at a nursing home. Chances are, you will keep up with your good deeds if you enjoy them.

epilogue

NOW THAT YOU'VE REACHED THE end of the book, I hope you realize there are lots of wonderful things about you, and I hope you've learned what you can do to be the best you can be. As you get older and have more grown-up feelings, just remember always to be the special, beautiful person you are from the inside out.

Marlene Wallach is the president of Wilhelmina Kids & Teens, a print and talent management company that represents newborns to teens in all aspects of print and broadcast media, including commercials, TV, and film. She strives to educate both children and their parents about the fashion and entertainment industries and to assist them as they navigate through a sometimes daunting business. As an author, she wrote a collection of four books published by Simon & Schuster and released in summer 2009: *My Self, My Life, My Look,* and *My Beauty.* At the core of these books is a message about empowering girls to find their unique beauty and have it shine from the inside out. "If one thing from one of my books helps one girl through the bumpy road of adolescence, the world is changed forever," says Marlene.

Real life. Real you.

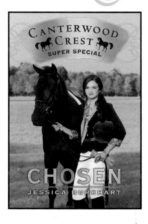

Don't miss any of these **terrific** Aladdin M!X books.